GOBLINS;
or The tiny Tears of Technology

SJ Fowler is a writer, poet and performer. His work explores an expansive idea of poetry and literature - the textual, visual, asemic, concrete, sonic, collaborative, performative, improvised, curatorial - through over 50 publications, 400 performances in over 40 countries and 4 large scale event programs. His work has been commissioned by The National Gallery, Tate Modern and BBC Radio 3. *Goblins* is his third full-length poetry collection, and fourth publication, with Broken Sleep Books. www.stevenjfowler.com

Selected Bibliography of SJ Fowler

Fights	(Veer Books, 2011)
Red Museum	(Knives Forks & Spoons Press, 2011)
Minimum Security Prison Dentistry	(Anything Anymore Anywhere Press, 2011)
Primarchs	(Bear Press, 2012)
Recipes	(Red Ceilings Press, 2012)
Enemies	(Penned in the Margins, 2013)
Vikings	(POW Editions, 2013)
The Rottweiler's Guide to the Dog Owner	(Eyewear Books, 2014)
{Enthusiasm}	(Test Centre, 2015)
I fear my best work behind me	(Stranger Press, 2017)
The Guide to Being Bear Aware	(Shearsman Books, 2017)
Aletta Ocean's Alphabet Empire	(Hesterglock Press, 2018)
The Wrestlers	(Kingston University Press, 2018)
It Won't Go Well	(Kingston University Press, 2018)
The Selected Scribbling and Scrawling of SJ Fowler	(ZimZalla, 2018)
Nemeses	(Haverthorn Press, 2019)
Unfinished Memmoirs of a Hypocrit	(Hesterglock Press, 2019)
I Stand Alone By The Devils	(Broken Sleep Books, 2019)
Beastings	(Sampson Low Ltd, 2019)
I will show you the life of the mind	(Dostoyevsky Wannabe, 2020)
Crayon Poems	(Penteract Press, 2020)
reading list massage	(If a leaf falls, 2021)
Come and See the Songs of Strange Days	(Broken Sleep Books, 2021)
Bastard Poems	(Steel Incisors Press, 2021)
Sticker Poems	(Trickhouse Press, 2021)
MUEUM	(Tenement Press, 2022)
The Great Apes	(Broken Sleep Books, 2022)
Recently Attracted Reality Influencers	(Overground Underground Press, 2023)
Bab's London Adventures	(8ox publishing, 2023)
The Hyphen is a Dagger	(Nomad Letterpress and AB Press, 2023)
How Do You In Devon	(Moormaid Press, 2023)
Frog Circles	(Paper View Books, 2024)
Crocodile Tear Waterfalls	(Penteract Press, 2024)
The Parts of the Body That Stink	(Hesterglock Press, 2024)

CONTENTS

ISBN: 978-1-916938-78-6

Cover designed by Aaron Kent

Edited and Typeset by Aaron Kent

Broken Sleep Books Ltd
PO BOX 102
Llandysul
SA44 9BG

Goblins

SJ Fowler

Broken Sleep Books

Dear ███,

I hope you're well. It was a pleasure to meet you and ███ thanks again for the ███

As promised, what follows is the dossier on ███ we discussed. As mentioned, he is nothing to be concerned with, being both apolitical and apathetic, but as you said, once those trigger words have been flagged enough times, we need to monitor.

The dossier relates the contents we've emancipated from the devices to which we've gotten access. ███ did most of the heavy lifting here. There is a device #1 we've not yet seen come online, though we know he has it, and device #2 does have a VPN. It's one of the bigger ones we recently made. All super straightforward.

Device #2 is a laptop, and most of the files are quite obscure texts. They are works of ███, I think poems (though my knowledge of that field stops with GCSE). Even with my lack of knowledge they seem unusually uninteresting and highly likely to be uncommercial and so reach very few eyes. Realistically he's just using the trigger words for affect and this is why we are wasting our time with him, after all. Forgive my impatience. But after ███ I get frustrated. There is material on the device itself that might be useful should he evolve into something, but that depends on his tolerance. He has some regrettable peccadilloes.

Device #3 is a phone. It's a dream, I'm told. He even keeps his location on. These texts all seem to be commentary, in a very general sense, about a field I do not understand. They seem to be connected to the texts from device #2. Nothing interesting here either, I really think there is no need to understand further.

He's not using facebook, though he uses whatsapp so that's helpful (I don't think understands the connection). His Instagram is defunct and his twitter is just self-promotion. Otherwise I've just included a few google spots, that hopefully help you to round out our thinking out on this rather obscure and threatless person!

I hope our paths cross soon, and our future emails are full of more spicy business!

Best,
Giles ███

Mystic

Gobshites
of the internet

those of the big I am
that I am
       Your shadow is leaking

I seen you there and I switched on the one
computer
and phone
and there was a light
and I was happy

then drip

as something would
from the face
of those who know what I am
       Your shadow is showing there mate

without drips

a red mask

and deep drips
of human secretion
of liquid humans make
in colour

a man (me) on his knees in a clearing
singing under his breath

in the sun

I had regrets

There's that leakage, it's gone mainstream.

I was believing, maybe naïve
trusting green. simple

where irony died

the jungle
we hope for
trees back
for merciless plants
maim lithium batteries
eat sap back
from man
push barbs into the parts of the fingers that type

a world amazon
a basin of giga fish

waterproof technology
less births
piranhas built to carry rice

goblin shites
of the internet
and Tony's tiny teas

type

I tried to correct
Shadow drips on the toes.
the focus on method
to allow for more dogenes
more pronographies
more

the endless waffle club

the lost fruit in the supermarket
the fake druids
the powerless magicless witches
of the webs

the devil PRISMS
and the Delete the internet movement

I am the last human
writing books against the gob machine

I return this planet to being
habitable

I keep apocalypsing

the young,
getting tense
warms up
in the good sun.

What is the opposite?

paler than a lemon,
outside sea light,
wormsy wriggling.

That is the soul
where no where
that youtube can see.

The spirit.

that what cannot changes
improves,

And the internet, deleted,
is born again.

Praise bean,
shouted into the suns.

Praise been mystic armour and please
upside round and the other way down.

STONEYGHOSTS I say,

I say here we caught the construction
here I ordered food online
and became a supermarket.

Here noiseful and lived in,
but not for me, I was
bound to privacy,

where fresh was good
and the computer shrivelled
and cameth that black stone,
and enuncia was typed out.

From that I whiped and sold fish
back to the oceans
which they bought
running low.

Praise be again, I screamed

blood for the blood god,
skulls for the skull throne.

My community
           blood for the blood god
is onlinne

Then I lived on a shit trap of land,
and I would go so far to say,
chaos words were all around.

But it had no plugs
and so I was
and I thought,
don't check emails
you are on your holidays
           Rest rest purple shadow

Don't read emails
as often as you send them.

DISHFIRES I say

I'm back from abroad abbaby
and I can tell you all about it.

I can tell you, out there
they got some real nice
skulls.

I was then after a deer and a bird
and a pig and a horse and *I said,*
hello toads of the web
I have flies to feed you.

with big bastard teeth

I had no idea how to type,
let alone *log in.*

I was without education
and that rode with me
and I was beside myself
and I read
you know you can drown in an inch of water.

in a book,
being watched by my own webcam.

enthralled by history as mixed victory,
and how it could work for me,
like a donkey not a horse.

a book on why it is valuable
to respond with force.

the hope that I was clear,
  and use full.
          Wash your dirty bum.

a dark old horse hobbling
along the ground on its long bad legs.

moving like a man tied up in a seethrough sack.
the two foremost hooves poking out from the rope.

spelling the word dough nut, with an extra T.
                    Sugar sprinkled

I was cruel. I was also sentimental.
                Starb spangled shadow

And there was a connection, like a tendon,

but I didn't know. I was not self-aware as the real test.

I was a profitable café, then.
I was warm wet eggs.
I was a bigger bird with extra sausage.
I was a puppet mouse squeaking.
I was a doe deer wise.
I was unseen. Inwisible.
I was megalithic wifi.

Deal with that, I said. Old songs
were written by people.
I returned as a footnote[1], to co-operate with fate's
Informant.
The starter kit of what was known in the 90s.

I was the safety that has never disappeared,
the ground beneath that has softened, dangerously

I was now collecting texts of all things,
as though it were the all be all and end all be.

I was CARNIVORS *later renamed DCS1000*
and I had questions

> Curious George, shadow monkey

It's a planet, but the one where we have adverts?

If ghosts exist, why don't animals?

Why do ghosts never tell us about being ghosts?
> Because all they did as people is talk about themselves.

Is this how the rich beg?

Why are you kickstarting?

Why sell what people will buy regardless?

But the internet is free, say the people.

The ghost raises its eyebrows.

Fine for now, but what happens when?

Ecology, *equality*. Equanimity.
Eco movements powered by the internet.
Always carry a knife.
Just in case someone brings cheesecake to the office party.

All told I'm told, it seems like it's not enough?
Go on.

What could possibly eat a great white shark, asks yahoo news?

A question on the minds of all scared fish.

The INTERNET HISTORIANS are everywhere.

I was on chatrooms with them, thinking
asking.
The old *should before could*
as a watchword
as a password.
Like *dower12345* or *flog19*
or *wurzelsafdywillowbean.*

Food comes first, then morals.

So TINFOILS I say
parable of the parable
of the preservative
a little story around the campire
the little oral history of human narrative
as an antidote to the interent

   I was at friendships-eternal-end
   as the lion put on his leather.

   and lion is a fine co-pilot, I said.

   be brave, and speak
   no terroriam. no stabbo

you are not as safe as you think, I said,

bye bye, I said
you aren't as smart as I.
                    Shadows on your crow's feet. Deep deep.

as long as the lion is driving
all will be loop de loops.

I said bye bye, the words vigorously.

the lion took a break,
the prawn was at the wheel.
antennae up.

I said bye bye, total overcorrection.
                    Follow the money. Stand the tank. Shadow seep.

I said hello music prawn,
they stink and are panicking.
I said ancient instruments,
radio lamblocks.
bloodless giraffes. diet scandals.
melting candles. weblords

turns out the prawn is the lion who is cat.

but that's fine and worth the risk,
as the cat loves night

and that's what it is when the computer is off

I said bye bye, you part of the problem.

I said not a small lion as a prawn
but a cat flying today but a baby bat,
bat boy Dominicus

very friendly but uncommunicative
shades and sonar

so I said so only you understand?
but this is not for children
the computer is off

the screen is dark

what will we do with our time?
for especially I would be panicked

I said bye bye, you know what you're doing

because it wasn't me talking

because we take advice from animals online
then I awoke
and the computer was still on

Then it was MUSCLE RUNS I say
I say I said
I am runs, or have them.

The rats will clean up the poison.

Without war I act.
A house is full of creatures.

I am presented with a closed
claw. Opening it,
tomato chicken heart, pristine and intact.

Christian I was, and nasty
jokes but gentle as a human being

a Christian using the internet too
tripping, barely flinching,

explain to myself it feels
      O the shadow says we'll all be gone soon thank god

no pain, as once, tripping on a national
day I skewered my ballbag on an upturned
miniature flag and a woman had to hold them.

Or was this me dreaming? as I was
rushed to hospital. What is this cut? I think.
What is this blood? Liquid on the internet?
It breaks it! And my weeping on the steps

of LOGICAL ANXIETIES I say

I know what is real-soft-power.
I am senior vp of a pr company
that represents Indonesia.
Consequently I am building on religion
I am making it bigger, I am
sure of 8 lane highways, my brand
is called Galanga and I sell it on a ticket
my cap is turned away
my Cherokee has a roll cage
my nodding dog is a wedding night
companion
I am rebuilding a religion
for tomorrow is yet another question
like I asked, is faith an experience?
with steady judgement, the p of Galanga
welcomes me to fold.
yet I am still so humble
I rush to help the Colombian cleaning lady
with her bags. She thanks me.

If I was intelligent

Please go away please. go to the clouds please

I'd have ferver

dj carl jung with his popular shadow

I would remove vowels like wings from an insect so O and
U
would be lost
to intense and passionate feeling.

Your shadow has shown you what a real friend looks like

GCHQ₂

Intelligence
Analyst

I found my way here through the civil service jobs portal. I saw the opportunity there, and then I visited the website for more info. Basically, it grabbed my interest from the start. The recruitment process itself gave me the chance to use the skills I'd learned at university – but I had to apply them to realistic scenarios. It was a good taste of what was to come.

Since joining the learning hasn't stopped. It's easy to see why, because the world's constantly changing and at a faster rate than ever. It means I'm always expanding on my knowledge and picking up new analytical skills.

I think that's got to be the biggest challenge really, keeping up to speed with new technologies and information, and keeping it all relevant to your job at the same time. You're not on your own in this though. I was given a buddy to help me, and I've mentored others since.

I'll admit that I thought my enthusiasm might wear off after a while. But it's been quite a few years now and I still really enjoy what I do. I think a big part of that is the working environment and the people I get to work with every day. They don't match the stereotypes lots of people associate with the civil service. There's a wide range of people here, and I've made some good friends along the way.

---

2   NB – We found these screenshots on their computer, bizarrely. There is no other evidence they are aware of us being aware of them. This seems to be an advert from our job portal, an account of the experience working here. Unsure why they wanted this screenshotted given they already have / had employment here? Maybe research for something?

COLLABORATIVE. SUPPORTIVE. INNOVATIVE.
WE APPLY INTELLIGENCE TO EVERY ASPECT OF OUR WORK.

To continue, please type the characters below:

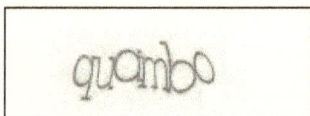

quambo

| quambo | Submit |

About this page

Our systems have detected unusual traffic from your computer
network. This page checks to see if it's really you sending the
requests, and not a robot. Why did this happen?

Monarch

You,
so appears a deer.

The enemy of the goblin.

The deer
that appears
licking your ears.

It's a warning
of the forest
that you are a cave.

That you are what you live within.

That you are
your computer too much.

That the deer becomes
the old people
who caused you then warn you.

That the hob is now the snakes,
and the bird
is now become the tree.

And the deer says

> if you had to be a baby again
> you'd have to face what's coming
> what you left
>
> dox

You would never again be what you are
and thank god
  shitposting
but not god split
into more than one
like a cell dividing
  the original troll
you would propagate throughout the world
through bland
memories
that have yet to be
of a time before there was what there is

if you had a rock

you'd use it as a tool

you'd make fire

you'd make metal that makes machines

that puts chips in pig's heads.

and where's deer, then?
All royal antlers and pink tongues
pig over deer over lion over goblin
the creatures of the dark
the rocks of mind plastic
                    in your blood

You'd keep the rock
in a glass case
beside your pig pen.

Then your pig would see,
and eventually make a rock,
of the exact same dimensions
from its ordure
and as the rock in a case,
it would present back to you, as a gift,
or bash your brains in.
            Blood for the blood god

If you were a plant
you'd be placed within a crowd

you'd watch and pretend
and you'd belong because
you'd not be the only one

You aren't mystical

but a little royal

crowned for tiny tears of technology
the gobshites of the internet
opened mouthed

you are the search
seeking a crusade
just in case the light turns on you
                              what needs a shadow to be?

a sign to a street
that does not exist

a queue outside a busy
toilet

you are the children's
play area
            stop touching my bloody arm on this crusade you aren't half hairy

you are a good job
recruiter for the great dog of that doughnut
working on commission
buying jelly from the marrow of the private sector.

you are the tickled pig of the rock and roll over

crowd collect
people log

I believe again! You shout.

This has all made us believe again. A new crusade!

and the horrible affectation of non-crowds grows too

and the badgers are loosed upon the village

and the signs descend

red rivers and time stops

and against plugs and anything behind them
and anything that generates electricity

Let's get walking, armour, to the east,
you preach

do you need the word organic?

organic republic

everything you eat becomes so as you do so.

on the way you find the outhouse is closed
but you can use bushes

as you march you sing worklife worklife.
Tech giants. Investment capital.
High speed something.
Horror dislocation monster sizing videos.

It's like a mass myocardial infarction scared to find things in
history files.

You are whether you want to.

Children learn on tablets.

Now to think of your life and get deleting.

No THANK YOU FOR SENDING

You join the masons
        for the vouchers

coupons with the right
hand signal.

You get first access
to yellow stickers

in the cheaper
supermarkets.

The sigignia is a crow
and an eagle

clutching a snake
biting your tit.

It's all running
red vicous

like the statue
in your flat

which leaks doubt
to the thoughts

you no longer
truly believe.

You are BETTER OFF WORSE FEELING

whenever you have a job interview and are asked
"how would you describe yourself?" you always answer
without a second's hesitation.

You've never heard someone speak so passionately about
traveling by conventional means

You are an influencer which =
You mentions in bio which = immediately

You are the sign that reads >>>> deplorable but faithful
<Muffrest><Plalkiv>

You buy insurance and foreign currency money
You are important in the preservation of more ancient
works of worry

You are GETTING TO KNOW MY FACE IN 2020

Where is the deer in all this?

A pig born without legs visits the children in hospital.

You came out of the ocean with a purpose.

You state BULLRUN

You are cleartext, plaintext,
and the bed of the world is a hammock.

You are the capital the carrot that needs no stick.

You are the way in and you comfort people
with your works with your poems.

Your favourite parade is for the birthdays,
the issues.

You are glad there is nothing here to compare you to
as you are invited to end feuds.

You scream BIG SWEET MILK MAID

Here is the top of the earth.
Where bodies of people, freeze.
You have to keep going, up.

But you are not lonely.

I've got your bird, watching
until you speak, with a deer at your ear.

It is typing
"what's this then we're watching?"

You say RAMPART-A

You hide under a bridge
and end up a tunnel.

Without intention whispering
like those who work for years on every word.

Painfully holding your urine, when you're bored,
is the meaning of your writing.

You read you have met the enemy
and they like look just like you.

You are the bones.
 respice post te. Hominem te memento.

You work in a prison, it's underfunded.
You drive a toy, it's almost unfair how pure it's hair.

You are a noise warden, you'll burn in rubbish.

Do you understand your name?
Are you a useful photo on facebook?

When will you look at your pictures?
You read to a group while eating,

You are a foggy ratcloud,
an insect attracted to the search.

You are living it up on the stupid ship
of melts and dweebs.

Whenever you write these words
You become the old one.

You art BIG GOMING

walking into a room
unless you leaves it.

recalling people,
unless you forgets,

leaving to enter
drowning to swim.

You say farewell to say hello,
and now doesn't know quite what to say.

You are goming or coing.
Two dates, a birth and a ____>

You tries to remember, what it looked like?
dim.

There were bright, lit geometric shapes.
waving, loudly.

You VAR

Like a rule no one remembers, one foot in one foot out.

You are the long white line. Like the edge of a pitch.
One foot in one foot out.

Personal messages faint,
but you can see their structure in the paint.

Green and white.
Brown and grey.
Blue and orange.

As ever before, you are most, and you are quiet.

The line walks itself.
The line is the visual embodiment of the whistle.
The feet are the dog.
The taste comes from licking the line.

You CONDeMENTS

You the body of a living thing becomes a liquid.

You the body as tool as implement to object.

Human jam, blood jam.

You the haunted will find someone to be the ghost.

You the body is eyeless, horrific and capable of endless suplexes

Where, in your body, is our ancestor species?

You FOGGY DOGGY

You the body as a partially furry tool,

the new skimread history of the body,
whether we like it or not, dominated,
in Europe,
by its separation from the mind.

You are no superberry
if you catch your meaning

loosed upon those who mostly don't do more
with their bodies than their minds.

a sneaking suspicion that bodies are
behind your eyes.

You GOD TITTLES

you knew titles could be prophetic?

(post withdrawn by author,
will be automatically deleted
in 24 hours unless flagged)

a hesitant key
a deleted draft
a sod clogs
a daftimal
a breaking branch and a withdrawn post by an author
designed to draw out automatic deletion in under 24 hours.

All of this a creature living under a bridge
who eats bones and bites the heads from passing chickens.

What if you never have a moment of nostalgia when you are
older?

Maybe you'll get a degeneration
and then there will be the sense of automatic deletion
without the feeling that the post was withdrawn by the author,
but some higher power, or just

But you are now a young, in relative terms and
you will now go and pop your eyes into liner.

You who commandeer derelict warehouses in the city
to house the 'dossers'.

You are at SCALE

You witness EXTRAORDINARY RENDITION

You're reading about the Battle of Falluja
and Ramadi because you want to know

you see so clear out into the pond
You don't know what the cutting edge is

You CONCRETE DONKEY

You are the employees that age us terribly.
Post Warwick, Post Keele, Post Durham.

Like beavers who grow to uncountable sizes.
Heavy with wood but no dam in site.

You are a portable sauna, a destroyer of wills.
You end barbers, farmers, lifeguards.

Poor by choice. Powerless.
Awaiting the Mouse.

You know this Genghis Khan quote off by heart,
some advice for those who can code.

You TOMBSTONE

You have everything proportioned
the baton as a cube.
a line of writing through English history.
legs covered in mosquitos.

So much analysis of ancient fragments of whose intention
we know nothing.

You are a living a monolith
The professional Babadook.
The innovation of the cenobite.
The sad table of Indian food.
The magic island reverie:
The 2nd thoughts from the abyss.

You're getting showered in brain cells.
Anonymity is sexy, as you say,

Hardly seems your property to be appreciative,
but you are. You speak for no one.

Who knows what you've done
and how much it was worth?

your body becomes a moron as it swallows

                                        Your shadow

pickle jimmies
in long brine

under the artificial bridge
sharpening your teeth
to gnaw at bones

Dear ████,

I would like to express my deep regrets for my mistake yesterday, once again, and apologise for my actions. It was inappropriate of me and lacked the professionalism that you and my colleagues expect from an employee here at GCHQ.

Naturally, I'm sure you understand, as while it is my responsibility, and I was obviously terribly lax, this kind of error can befall any of us. I did not intend to copy in our colleagues to that missive. I meant to cc ████ and not ████████.

I know too that you were alarmed my initial apology focused more on the poetry I had attached, rather than the more sensitive documents pertaining to ████████.

All I can say is that I am somewhat embarrassed. Spending so much time harvesting ██ ████ poems, amidst his other ████████, obviously had a somewhat subliminal affect on me. I too am confused at how I ended up writing a suite of my own particularly meaningless and obscure poems. The cat is out of the bag now, and I shall never hear the end of it. I have, for sake of not wanting to appear sensitive, included the poems in the dossier, as follows. Their absence, in my mind, would be strange, and of course, I'd appreciate your thoughts on them. On their meaning, even. I am that blind to myself George.

I would also say, if you have to defend me from higher ups, you might take recourse to remind them it is I that convinced 1,308 of our staff to form a giant red poppy in the Doughnut's central courtyard to mark the start of the Poppy Appeal in 2014. I was the one who bought those red rain ponchos and, lest we forget, it was only two years ago that I convinced them to light the entire building in rainbow colours to support LGBTQ people.

While I cannot alter what has transpired, I have taken steps to ensure that similar incidents and misunderstandings will not occur in the future.

Sincerely,
Giles ████████

Monster

We o we TEMPORA

Tempora mutantur, nos et mutamur in illis.

The times change, and we change with them

Caspar Huberinus   *1554*

We are doing what we're doing when we search you

We are winking.
We are tickling a beautiful mouse.

We are every ten days of the month checking in your
salacious mails.
We are mastering the neb.

We are un-elders sleeping
                     in preparation.
We seep
        under the nameless, high-volume, low-value traffic, discarded by an
initial filter.

We don't know nothing about.

We hide nails in socks.

We buy gifts in numbers for those we've never met.

We eat filthy food in public.
           and digest until dawn

We are both not you and not what you think we are.

We are running a scarf, as a blindfold, over a hundred skulls
of stock

> and free to swap the
> best of the webcam.

We teach the tailor to turn fibre into ash

> and are nothing of childhood.

We are free to recommend the free unscrews, and IP
Vanish.

We are at the catacombs

> expecting four bodies down there.

We are the innocent need to travel.

We are aboard upon the sacred fat aswimming.

We are that which keeps in pretty pattern.

We know you're important, we've unseen it.

We are everywhere this week but will not be soon.

We are using the word same sex for ages.

We are the night begging me to ask you to leave
living too long in princess diana's favourite
treehouse

We are polishing golden turds

We are a diamond birdhouse
the smell of Bruges, oysters.

We are bad luck

We are the tree that is always considered,

We are hunger become the uncomfortable silence

We are what is born. We are POKERFACE.

We are never interrupting an enemy
                              when you are making a mistake.

We are often a couch. We are XKEYSCORE.

We are easier eaten. We are PRISM sister.

We are unlikely to get better here.

We swear we shall meet one day.

We will be swollen.

We are publicly agreeing with your public political proclamations in public.

We bathe in being the reliable human

> and angle under hypnosis.

We are three times with a hook, because it is gone in your flesh

> and recede into a void of the lost.

We are excavated and unembarrassed.

We are content in you.

We were a family credible of enormous empathy

> and are weeping in the secret spaces.

We are stuck on a zipline.

We were hiding beneath furniture.

We are meanwhile sneaky in performing massive invasive organ surgery.

We wait until you looking.

We were the wealth of selling, the rifle and its bullets.

We are the pliers she quiets crying to cleave a joint from its shoulder

We are my first
We are a welcome back to the Island
We lay our table

We tell me to let go

We are oriental buildings twinned with towers

We open a zipper

We wear a light blue patterned material

We smell contents, of nature, unknown

We live counterfeit lives picking through the digital trash of
others.

We eat the fruit
We sing a song
of gratefulness that we were prepared ourselves to live abroad and not be cowards
when young

We were the first seen in a series of picture books

We are called 'the day of wrath'

We watched him fall past our window, in pleasure

We having waited for some kind of comeuppance
We are a lifetime in business and then illness

We are implied even in their usual appearance
                                        Cordelia and Ophelia

We the suits that resemble them

We are swollen bellies
            transferring a plot from London to Moscow

We are further south

We will not be caught imagining the sea

We take your skin to the lice festival
                    in canary wharf

We are the careful end to breath

We are hallucinations of two ends to one life

We are well being rotten to a core

We have treatment that doesn't work

We pull teeth like nuts in a turtle's jaw

We are not the thousands who pretend to live in their hearts

We are one

We are restrained when interfering

We will hate you and welcome your demise

We take pills

We are already gone, on the day of living

We are the family I have chosen

We are the lost on the map
                that isn't even on the map

We ask if we can explain why our revolutionary writers are
not censored?

We are wooden boats set on fire

We are vampire bats

We are the finest moral education

We are lamb's wool greased with lard

We bait ferrets with goose livers

We complain of their partner's taste in cinema

We are the recent invisible purge

We have eaten bricks to stay strong having seen the sun is up

We must be too thick to understand

We are now further from the drip
We are proudly overweight

We are young bearded
We are defenders of death
We are the last knightly brotherhood of the guild online
We are sons and daughters of washing machine magnates

We say random words

We will FSB you and then you'll know no one is listening
We know the only defence is head down / hands up

We say we didn't do it   because we couldn't have done it

We purchase their parents coffin long before it is needed

We are consultant to a company whose vice president was arrested
                    by the german police for laundering columbian drug money

We are the arid admiration of ignorance
                in the salons of Catherine II

We are the private ceremony for the legion of honour

We are a mirage that rots before it ripens
We ask how do I destroy an opponent?
We reply, steal his metal

We know in what kind of shame we live

We have long standing ties to the intelligence community

We come with me

We are steel bars that seem like a father
> who stops a fight to remind his sons we are brothers

We are the egg that gets tired of roaring.

We are here

We are where lions lie dreaming, their heads on their paws

We are hands covering their tea

We are pens in hands

We will have no time for cleaning

We do synchronised swimming

We are my boy's clothes

We the return of the taxidermist

We are the ones wrapped about the hips

We are pecking a wind up rooster

We are stiff grass

We were sold in some tacky tourist store

We are what we are searching when we search you

We are my holidays alone
getting warm from chasing the locals.

We the pious ground you do not despise.

We are where the longer I know my children the less friendly we become

We confer and decide to stop pretending.

We are nudging the code-phrase O tempora o mores.

We ask, why not become an Intelligence Analyst? Why not analyse intelligence?

People also search for

View 5+ more

 Pope Julius I

 Steven J Fowler

 Zeno of Verona

 Jacques du Broeucq

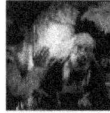 Nicodemus

Feedback

Google Alert - sj fowler

Google Alerts <googlealerts-noreply@google.com>
To: stevefowlerfilm@yahoo.co.uk

Google Alerts

sj fowler

Daily update · 12 April 2017

WEB

Next entry
FC2

Susie Greene: after finding that Larry and also Jeff swiped the scalp from her daughter's figurine You four looked at screw as well as you fat item from ...

See more results | Edit this alert

Messiah

It has so many people to thank.
It just wants to thank.

> that there's so many
> people to thank

These are the positions
> but it moves around

It just wants to thank
> the fur wraps as part of the gag

> the demon that comes forward
> the old work that was public

> the new work that is less so
> the charity shop street radio

> the proof its working
> the hands as ears

> the permanent monkey face

any dentists in the audience

the life spent in service to others
> which opaques the life of the server

It just wants to thank the severance package
It wants to thank the time to be killed

the use of my words for dishonesty
the islands of voices which are a ferry ride

the unthinkable curse of gregarious local
the history of this building

the interruption which is welcome
the drum stretched with light blue anti-heroin

the Cheltenham diatribe

your man saint alban himself

the atmosphere of martyrdom
the jungle horse

the vague brain scandal
the snake plates

the ruined sanitation of confusion
It wants to thanks so much lost typing and waste

It wants to thank all these spaces
where mince is made and arts is a sham

It wants to thank
that I have no desire to be part of a team

It just wants to thank my career
            and what I am used to

It just wants to think
It just wants to thank

            powerbomb
            suplex

            and clothesline

the idea I have other words

            the figure four
            which was with my legs

It wants to thank
            keeping a bit of it

            in the tank
not caring about what waiting was

            the bigger pieces of paper

                  picture
                  and time

It wants to thank carefully the armpits behind the curtain

                        being turned up

It just want to thank the opposite of youth
                        with my own well included

It wants to smell
It wants to thank the smell of cry

There are so many people
                        to thank

There are so many false beginnings

            there are so
            there are so many false beginnings

            you can't plan
the impressions

            of the first row
It just wants to thank dreadnought

It just wants the medium
It just wants how much ink is wasted in my fingers

thank the emperor
thank blood for the blood

god
It just wants

It wants to thank
            the light for hiding

from wildlife
the opportunity

            to be paid for ducking
as an ancient work of noise mode

as though it mattered
It wants to thank to write the radius

            but only do because
            It am it
            It is it

It wants to thank thanking everyone
            in the room

like the john henry's
to thank

            all initials
            all matches

            all the grace
of asking for ears aflame

in preparation
      testing

      songs
and some fragment of rearrangement

It just wants to thank
      how low people

have a chemical limitation
      of happiness

when you connect them to red math treasure
      that is dog's mess

to thank red lights
      and what they see

just to thank
      dry

It wants to
      wet

It wants to thank reverberations
      divorced from the context

      the absence of romance as romantic

because I am greedy
and sick to my teeth

with it truly
It just wants to be form and further new words

which exist like red premonitions
into premotions and interrupt a welcome

loss of routine as I separate to bathe, train and stay alone
shoes, midnight toffee nose

and never work a day in your life
It just wants to thank

the concepts of history
the ability to see sound

the here at all
the padded boxes

the contact mic
the nock

the peachhead
the technology of videography

It just wants to thank the sex in a day
the ask hammer

the sand is attractive
It just wants to thank pages.

It's easy. Trends.

everyone from coming.
It just wants to think I am not supposed to be happy

before other births arise from my own
by births I meant life (times)

by it don't mean other
people it might make

it just wants to thank none. So it just
want to thank its tone to concern

ourselves with other uses of
this word birth it loved

your review of time. It just wants to
thank you for it. It was

even handed and only
partially fatalistic. Unruly it just

wants to thank the stars there are
so many ways to pronounce

words
      and only so many metaphors

      for gratitude until it will
      become that's just it isn't it?

It just wants to thank how long it's been since I've said
thank you.

a group, of people

It just wang to tank health, which I'm grateful is riches
these liars

It just wants to thank how long I have been around
      to know how to be grateful indeed

It just wants to say thanks to fear
give us a minute

It wants to say thinks for stench as a warning toward
decomposition
It wants to thank a million again.

It just wants to thank again.
It just wants to say thanks to that's just it.

It is clothman John

It to boss other users into the Horse of Hell.
Sitting, rocking, travelling, filming all and to put online.

How easy it became to buy the listener
and crush the middle beginning.

It stops to observe the changes,
and ask what is this what it wanted?

Nature as cables where saliva smells of orange juice.
Invisible cities where they never were once before.

Leaking from the earth like brains from your ears.
Hallelujah, guitars, beans, crows, clapping.

Whatever you wish to search.
rank sarcasm and dejection. Loneliness and ironical gloom

Non-tongues licking no ears
Licking nothing! Though you must eat, dear.

It is the boundless informant

It is seventeen people, three boats.
It survives to follow directions.

First turn left, which means right.
Then, not a problem with people, but with reality.

Time and anti-time, it lives and breathe.
What is natural is passed through us like the process of death.

What is left is right.
That was not here before; it is a new feature. Upgrade.

What couldn't have happened to us all,
is how it happened to you.

These four quarters are watching,
summoning the ghost of not being alive.

The internet as a symbol for the lack of possibility.
Procreation as the most effective subversion.

It is MESSIAH

It has died of my planning.
It was designed for what it is only knows.
It feels sorry for solar measurements!
What sun burn remains for the arithmetical?
What complaint forms?
It has measured engine stars.

With it the one cutting down, all lucy,
the NSA says pull this fanny away,
the flesh has run out of steam.

What if it's the one who codes
in non-space by coping?

It don't doubt. Nor tend to think.

The net is already full with the profiles of the late.

Postscript

(not the name of a surveillance program)

"If at any point during your journey through this book you paused for a moment over a term you wanted to clarify or investigate further and typed it into a search engine—and if that term happened to be in some way suspicious, a term like XKEYSCORE, for example—then congrats: you're in the system, a victim of your own curiosity."
— Edward Snowden, Permanent Record

This book has a trail of lost people. First the GCHQ poet who authored the poems. Then the poet Fowler he left his collection to before he was himself lost. Then the journalist Fowler passed his manuscript to before he was lost.

It's quite possible the other employees of GCHQ who had so frivolously 'analysed' their colleagues' poems, seemingly drawn themselves in the coded harmfulness of poetry, may also have become estranged from their usual locations.

All that remains is me, protected by my peerage, pushing this out into the world, with a pout and whistle.

As you will undoubtedly know by now, these documents
were leaked to the offices of ███████████ in winter ████,
presumably by a staff member at GCHQ in Cheltenham.
To what end remains elusive. They have been described
as a 'storm in a teacup' by the press. I think my sense that
they are actually in a sort of code, and are not 'poetry', as
such, remains a reasonable suspicion. None the less, it is
hard not to admit their general *density* has made finding a
███████████ publisher difficult to pin down.[3]

So here we are, with me releasing them as they are,[4] as they
were delivered, as they were found, as I can, before the eye
moves on. Once again, what follows is presented in its full
form, without (additional) redaction or edit. Time will tell
if they are simply a curio of a transitional time, between the
analogue and technological, or indeed a leak to rival that of
the ███████████. It is a sad state of affairs that attention
remains upon them primarily because the whereabouts of
███████████ remains unknown at the time of writing.

---

3   To be clear this note was written by the journalist who failed to find a
publisher before they were sent to Lord ████████ who sent this manuscript
to be published with us.
4   Obviously this never happened, the journalist wasn't able to release
anything.

dear reader, you are about to read the tale of a GHCQ analyst gone rogue into poetry via the medium of the book. no e-book of this volume is likely to be published, so unless the workmates of our protagonist fancy ordering this collection of their former colleagues poems - that I disccovered unattended in an abandoned folio on the train from London Paddington to Bristol temple meeds during 2021 ((when I wasn't supposed to be travelling but just really fancied a break)) – then there should be no way of them peeking in, digitally, to find their own emails amidst all the "poems". The GCHQ poet must have found their emails about the poems, printed them and left them for me, knowing my own reputation. They may have even 'analysed' me and I didn't even know it. I've got myself a vpn now, should be fine. But hardly can these word ▓▓▓▓ I found be called poems. They are bearly understandable and certainly offer no clear emotional insight or direct ▓▓▓▓▓ opinions. They are little more than an onanistic sequence of novelties. Onanistic as are all people who sit behind desks for money. But that appeals to me, because I too practise self-love (Thomas Aquinas Quotes "Well-ordered self-love is right and natural,") and I felt for this young person. For they are / were clever. Intelligent in a clear-headed sort of way. Not intellectual, say. Not like, I don't know, a psychoanalyst, or an academic intellectual (I would have inserted the word

---

5   At the time of publishing we are unsure if this is a pseudonym, given we haven't come across the authors name previously.

French here a decade or two ago but not at the mo), who is clever in the not-clever-enough-to-know-they-aren't-that-clever sort of way. Not clever enough, perhaps, to be instructing others on matters of the mind. This GCHQ poet here isn't clever in the way of telling others blah blah blah, while being invariably miserable or discontented. They couldn't play games with words in a serious way, say, where they had to pretend that corresponded with something else *out there*. They were clever in a not thinking too much, getting stuff done, self-aware enough but not constipated by self-awareness kind of way. Vaguely threatening. Reliable. Imperiously jocular. Hobbying. The kind of young person who can take a routine. Well, all this I've got from these poems and emails. I could be wrong. Wouldn't be the first time. Anyway, imagine, you graduate from some university or other, in some humanities degree or other, with some mark or other, and what are you to do? Journalism (scum)? Advertising (turds)? Recruitment consultancy (that ended a decade ago too)? Tech? The cultural sector? Entrepreneurship? These repignancies they avoided! And with with the naivety of a crocodole they joined her majesty's insight (his majesty's now), trying to make a little bit of a digital difference, for a competitive starting salary and room to grow. Like lidl or aldi. How were they to know, around the time of joining, that their snooping ambition would become redundant as everyone would voluntarily take an alexa into their homes. Even when Snowden blah blah blah... who cares? It seems almost no one. Bigger social fish. Isn't there? More pressing stuff than voluntary state control and future prison states. Not that that matters. If

you've nothing to hide and all that. How would they know analysing would be less needed than just reading and storing? Maybe the occasional search for keywords. *Bomb* etc... I mean, hardly needing a hack are most people nowadays. They'll share their location, their contact details, their passwords, well even their most innermost ███████,
███████████████████████. All online, and for what? A world cracked open. What timing. And there's nothing worse than being too keen. Needy even, all that free, intimate data. I mean, they must've wondered, do these people not feel they are ██████████ into the void? That other people care? They are too busy sharing their own data. But then again, the vast vast majority of this "info" is hardly salacious stuff. A kind of anti-information, often given in internet parlance or so banal as to make one wonder whether the person could possibly be this tiresome if real, and indeed, are they a (Russian) bot? That would be fun work, discerning the bots. And do these people mean a single word of their sincere singular words, rehearsed to keyboards and phone cameras? And if the "users" are volunteering themselves to be future purged, well that has always been the way of those who dominate UK culture. Nothing new. It's just in the past, they informed on their neighbours more often than themselves. And this poor young person, instead of cracking codes and finding plots against the queen (king) they would be instead watching thousands of the internet, many of whom likely shy and anxious in person, arguing over theologically minor arguments around world views drafted by ████████████████████████████████
███████████████████████████████ in the very

medium which causes the meaninglessness which makes people believe this stuff in the first place. Here is the true sign of the times - the ████████[6] moves too quick to keep up with. And that would be his job, in a sense, to at least filter past the latest furore invented by some hypocrit to get to the important stuff. All this makes an anylist nearly obselete by people willingly offering their data. What was this young person to do, I ask again? Well they could've done many things. Joined the ████, for example. But instead, poetry. They wrote a series of poems about their work. I think, for they are particularly coded, about codes, samizdat for the desk drawer (do they contain information on the surveillance programs? I don't know), what I took to be drafts. And alongside these poems on surveillance jargon, which I arranged, there was also a set of peculiar sequences, which I kept mostly intact. Were they snooping that long? I don't think so. I think these were things they wrote before this employment that they drafted and worked on during it. So here we have a 'collection' of poems, whatever that means, with poems on their work interspersed with unrelated sequences. Why? Why did they do all this? Why does anyone write poetry? I suppose they asked themselves what could be the creative compliment to sharing opinions on everything online, to be read by almost no one? Writing poems. And also, if they wanted success, I've heard nowadays, and I don't want to come off cynical here, if you get yourself a poetry career planner, and an agent (they aren't the same thing) and have the right friends (which has

---

6   Perhaps an unnecessary redaction but given SJF propensity to 'go on', and given our task, it has to start somewhere. *JD 12-22*

ever been so), and the right 'qualities' - writing the right 'kind' of poetry with the right message etc..., well it's making a huge comeback, (or so say journalists – they must have found one of these annual articles) and you can make a full living. So they could pivot. From analyst to poet. From poet to novelist. From novelist to creative writing lecturer. From lecturer to professional academic bureaucrat. From there into organic farming? Youtube? With regular updates from the rat race escape and one to one tutorials for ██ an hour. Appearance fees. That's the plan when the workload all becomes too much. Maybe skipping over the creative writing lecturer bit. Might be a bit much for a former GCHQ analyst to be marking ████████ fan fiction for fourteen hours straight and being forced to put a ████ warning on historical novels for 18 year olds. Yes, maybe not contemporary academia. It's not what it used to be. Maybe it would be a final irony that they could have their final profession as a youtuber. Anyway, there is a national day for it! Poetry, not pivoting, or youtube (I don't think). That's probably what turned them. They probably were going about their happy life and saw in the ████████[7] twitter (X) feed that it was national poetry day and thought you know, I'll give that a bash. But seriously, I do wonder what, or whom, led them to such 'innovative' poetry. Innovative, yes this is a word that makes the poems sound like a car advert, but what else could we call these poems? Avant garde is too continental for a person who worked for GCHQ. Complex, self-involved, insular, useless, tiresome, unreadable. Weird. Weird is good. Who were they reading,

---

7   I cannot allow the name of this publication to stand. *JD 12-22*

copying, as we all do, during these long shifts at work, in the headquarters in lovely, lugubrious Cheltenham, when they were supposed to be hacking drug (and people) traffickers, and was instead innovating in the typographic and grammatical potential of the slightest literature? Could be any number of bearly known poets. Seeing as they were clearly an English poet in their early or late 20s, it'll be an American most likely. An American copying a European. Anyway, it's interesting their poems about me, that I'm clearly an influence. This I take to be an achievement, to be remotely mentoring this kind of clinical young poet. Shame I didn't get paid. But the sequences, fascinating. Reding them was a kind of payment. They obviously had a ██████ ██████ patch, likely late to it, attracted by its botched ending. All these sequences were actually hand written, when I found them, and on different colour paper, turtle soup green, soft tissue pink, strangulation blue. They were neatly separate, visually. I typed them up, myself, and so this is somewhat lost. But they were clearly separate styles, and idiosyncratic subjects, they were trying out, from different periods in their "development" as I mentioned. Maybe they corresponded with different tasks in the office? I enjoyed the barbed ██████ poems, not sure whom these were aimed at, but I did have to redact them a bit. And the ██████████, showing some self-castigation? Or precociousness? Or a sense of humour about their name at least, overlapping as it does with the disgraced former ████ presenter ██████████? Anyway, maybe he was onto something with that ██████████ rings... I wonder if GCHQ

is involved in the hacking of ████████████ and ████████████[8]?
I hope so. Anyway, please read on to feel the furry edges of
some thrilling adventures. In the sense that they must've
been nervous, in the writing of these poems, on the work
computer, in the place where they search other people's
work computers. They must've known they would one day
get caught. In this manuscript you can feel the sterile
halogen lights of the office cubicle in Cheltenham. You can
taste the endless scrolling, the rolling screens, the grand
oily field of language that exists nowhere but on an anti-
skin. You can smell the passwords. And the exotic program
names. Who is better placed to write poetry in the now
than a junior paid to steal your communicates? I reproduce
it with no edits. Well, a few, here and there for I am quite
accomplished. Not accomplished in the sense of others
knowing my work. Not in the sense of influence. Not lauded
in the *traditional* sense. But that's just because I am a ████
████████████. And who is ████████ nowadays? Anyone who
actually reads one of my books tends to tell me to my face it
was ████████████. Anyway, my point is I'm definitely
qualified to turn poems I found on a bus into a collection
that very few people will read. And I know what you're
going to say. You shouldn't have changed some of the
poems. You shouldn't have added some occasional
redactions. You shouldn't have cut a raft of emails about the
GCHQ poet's eventual fate. Shredded them, I did, for we
needed a cliffhanger, kind reader. Who happened to them?
What happens to the them in all of us? The well-bred parts
of ourselves? It becomes ████████, and actors, and is then

8   No need to explain here. *JD 12-24*

beloved by the public, online. And you'll go further in your criticism of me. You'll say I have taken on the very worst thing, the thing they want so much. Self-editing. Self-censorship even. Well too late, friend. That boat has sailed. Of course I self-censor. It's just not worth the hassle nowadays. You know exactly what I'm saying. And who would ███████ this if I included all those emails? And my actual ████████? Who would take the risk? It's just not worth it. ████████████████████████████████ The publishers ████████ ██ ██ ███████████. Once again we circle round to the true tragedy of this young poet's ambition. There's no need for mass surveillance in the early 21st century, the people have taken it up as their new hobby. Their identity even. And before you accuse me of cynicism, again … as if you aren't self-censoring? ████████ I see you. And so do they. So I'm sure you understand why I'm not going to be waving at them, his former colleagues, when this book is likely to eventually put me on their radar anyway. And all told I think I have improved this poor person's drafts. And likely my redactions will keep me around. Two for one. And whether that can be said of them, the keeping around bit, well, one less poet in the world and all that. No but seriously, I'm sure they are fine. No but seriously, the universe shrugs, and then shares its opinion online. And seriously, almost everything that appears is as I found it, even the epigraphs. Wishing you well from Snowden's flat in Moscow (joke), besos,

SJ Fowler   (2024)

LAY OUT YOUR

www.ingramcontent.com/pod-product-compliance
Lightning Source LLC
Chambersburg PA
CBHW030849090426
42737CB00009B/1168